For Shari, Ethan & Helena

"Alone we can do so little.
Together we can do so much."

— Helen Keller

The Co+Factor

The Exclusively-For-Everyone, Not-To-Be-Kept-Secret Ingredient/Benefit
For Helping You and Your Organization Create, Engage and Prosper

By Scott Abbott

Rhymes & Reasons

Greetings & Salutations –

First and foremost, I hope all is good at work and life!

For the record, this little book, and moreover, **its purpose** - is to thoroughly **encourage** and absolutely **support** everyone who wants to improve and make things better, regardless of their current situation or circumstances (props, kudos, and fist-bumps - if that is you).

On the flip side, it's also intended to **challenge**, and frankly, maybe even **provoke** (he writes with a good-hearted wink ;), all of the complacent naysayers, cowering in the peanut gallery, who choose not to improve and make things better … because of fear, uncertainty, doubt, excuses, distractions, or other lame-duck, pass-the-buck, shortsighted, momentary rational.

(psst: if that's you, the good news is, **it's not too late to change**: nope).

Moreover, it's incredibly amazing, and just boggles the mind - that there are still people (in big-time positions) who think that "**business-as-usual**" is the preferred way to go. Really?!

Even more of a head-scratching bummer of an irony … is when knuckle-head, stuck-in-the-mud people … who use knee-jerk, reactionary, front-loaded, "I'll believe it when I see it; that's not the way we do it" **attitudes/temperaments/paradigms** … are actually paid and/or hired by their customers to help them (yes, their customers) "**think-out-of-the-box**," and do something new and different and probably expensive (like buying their products/services).

And while that close-minded, ignorance-is-bliss, totally uncool, and highly inappropriate thinking might not **impact them or their employers** now - chances are, that in time - it will.

Stay tuned; you'll see.

Furthermore, while I full-heartedly agree with a **tempered**, **methodical**, **diligent** approach to **rationalizing**, **assessing**, **debating** and **proving** new ideas, strategies, plans, and programs (you know, like the one that's in this book) - it's pretty darn difficult to rationalize, assess, debate and prove - if you can't even get the proverbial swing, let alone an at-bat.

I guess in those circumstances, the old adage, "**that it's hard to teach someone something new, when their job depends on not knowing it**"- **is true**. Though frankly, I think that in the not too distant future (like today) - that the opposite will hold true.

Time will tell.

The fact of the matter is (or should be), that some jobs will and should be lost, if/when the so-called "leaders" who do the decision-making, don't take the time to properly rationalize, debate, assess and prove - before saying no (or yes, for that matter). No news flash there, right? **After all, it's not just about you, or us as individuals, per se**: it's about doing what's in the best interest of the entire organization, and its **employees**, **customers**, and **partners**.

But you get that, don't you. **Sure you do.** However, if you work with someone who doesn't, and worse, is getting in the way of **doing what's right for the organization** - than please forward this to them. Consider it our **mutual civic and fiduciary responsibility**.

With **sincere appreciation** for **choosing the right path**.

And doing the right thing (with **happiness**, and **goodwill**).

Carpe Diem.

Scott Abbott

P.S. **Have Fun** & **Enjoy** :-)

"The **Why**"

As you probably know already …
there's this big-time, major-league,
better-make-it-happen-or-be-left-behind

initiative

that's **transforming** business (and pretty much our entire world, for that matter).

It's quite the buzz, actually:
From Corporations, to the Corner Shop;
Board Rooms, to Break Rooms;
Wall Street, to Main Street;
Schools, to Governments;
and everywhere in-between.

And Why?

Because it's more than just an **initiative.**

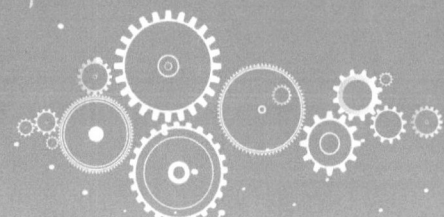

It's a

must-have,
real-world,
super-important,

directive
charter
mission
mandate

that given the **challenges** and **opportunities** of business today ·······▶

can make or break our individual and collective

SUCCESS AT
Work & Life

It's true.

And that

initiative
directive
charter
mission
mandate

is ... drum roll please ....

MOBILE SOCIAL

(#bemobileworksocial)

BE MOBILE

Innovative, growth-oriented organizations embrace (better yet, realize) the significant benefits gained by bringing all stakeholders (employees, customers and partners) together to strengthen engagement: whenever/however the stakeholder wants, using their favorite mobile devices. Whether elevating collaboration, enhancing brand awareness, driving customer acquisition strategies, streamlining business processes, or boosting sales and service - you can accomplish more (for less) by putting and keeping your business in constant flexible motion.

WORK SOCIAL

"Working Social" (on both an enterprise and individual basis) can drive increasing levels of collaboration and productivity, foster more effective relationships, and enhance how the market learns about, interacts with, and purchases your products and services. Social is not a passing consumer, corporate or institutional fad. Rather, it is a powerful and pervasive "way" through which you and your organization must consider its fundamental tenets: how it interacts with its stakeholders, and how it creates, develops, delivers, engages and monetizes its solutions.

THE BENEFITS OF BOTH

Together - mobile and social answers to the major societal, technological and economic shifts that are defining (if not driving) business, work and life: today, tomorrow, and beyond. With a structured and comprehensive mobile/social strategy, you can market and sell more effectively; enhance teamwork and collaboration; crowd-source (and supply) input, ideas and creativity; spot trends sooner; elevate meaningful interactions, loyalty and trust; optimize performance; build and maintain stronger teams; personalize motivation, and best of all ... grow better, faster, bigger, stronger, happier – for less time, hassles and costs.

"The **What**"

While there are a plenty of

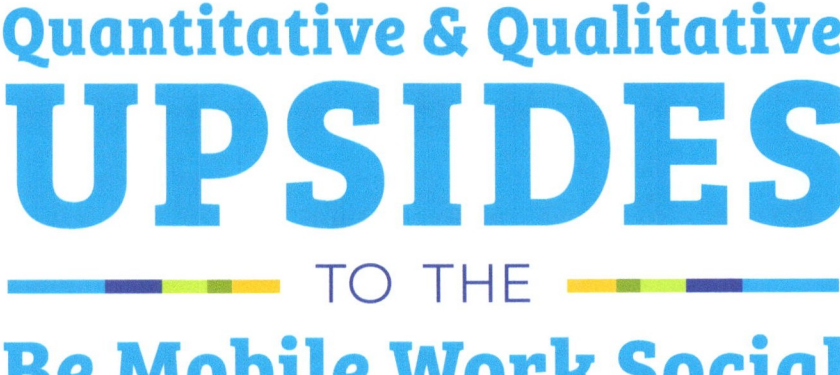

Quantitative & Qualitative

UPSIDES

TO THE

Be Mobile Work Social

Value Proposition...

one of the major **benefits (and drivers)** is/can/should be:

The Co+Factor

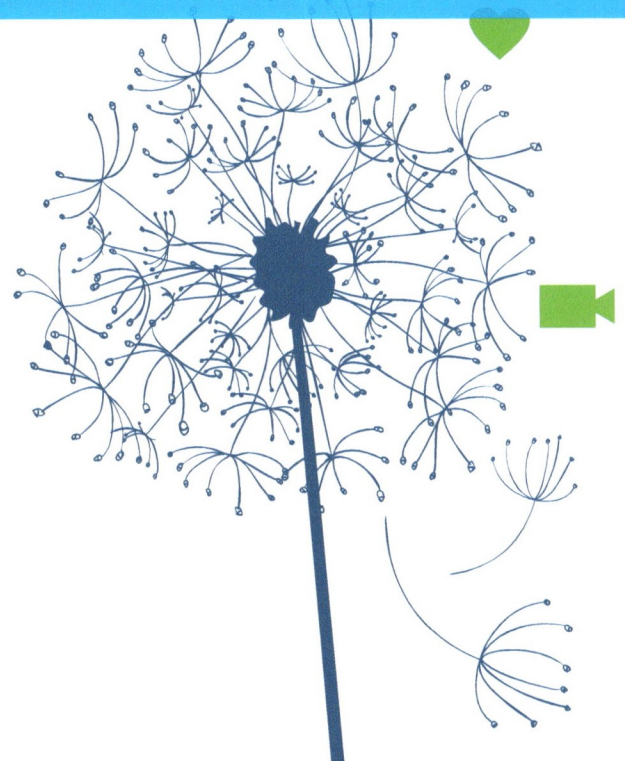

The Co+Factor is what you (can/should) get when you
blend, incorporate & leverage
the-best-of-the best, action-oriented, make-the-world-a-better-place

"**co**" words, like:

connected
collaborative
communicative
cooperative
compassionate
cohesive
coordinated
community

into an **authentic,**
unified, ➞ mindset
purpose-driven

mindset
philosophy
mantra
culture

that leverages the collective **knowledge**, **talents**, and **capabilities** of your **employees, customers and suppliers** (aka stakeholders) in order to help your company

operate
engage
grow
prosper ➞ **better than ever before.**

True again.

But ... if you happen to think it is easy to

establish, achieve and maintain

the tangible and intangible upside benefits that having

The Co+Factor

can/will/should produce ...

THINK AGAIN.

BTW: The Co+Factor also advocates other great co words like consciousness, considerate, comradery and comfort, especially when corresponding with cookies and coco. Moreover, feel free to use your own compatible and constructive co words; the Co+Factor is always copasetic with that kind of competitive co-creation ... especially if they're constructive, conducive, courteous, collegial and drive a Corvette. On the flip side, do your best to stay clear of the bad co words (yes, they exist too; it's a yin/yang thing) like: contentious, complacent, conspirator, combative, contaminated, cowardly, conniving cop-outs. Those words, and those that embrace them, are confusing and certainly not cool.

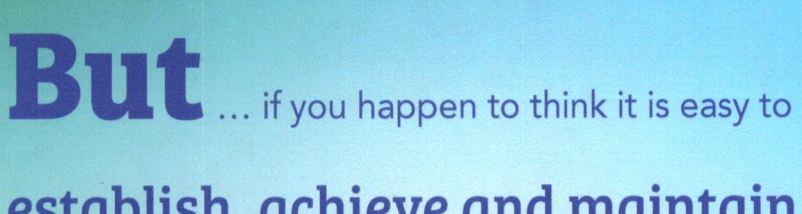

"The **How**"

To establish, embrace and optimize **The Co+Factor** – it will take equal parts **brains, brawn** and **heart** – framed, powered and supported by

"Systems of Engagement"

{**Systems of Engagement** incorporates/leverages a blend of mobile, social media, enterprise social networks, and legacy IT. But unlike traditional "back-office" **Systems of Record**, Systems of Engagement can/should generate a multitude of active, "market-facing" benefits-to-revenues … including a more cohesive, collaborative and engaged community of employees, customers, and partners … working in a more accessible, enjoyable way.}

that will help

guide
direct
unify
support
deliver

Your
Be Mobile
Work Social
+ Strategy
+ Tactics
+ Operations
+ Execution
+ Rewards

Furthermore …

IT. TAKES.
WORK.

Hard work even.

But when done well …
moreover, when enthusiastically …

Led
Established
Positioned
Infused
Adopted
Measured
Managed
Developed &
$$Monetized$$

Today's effective leaders use "social-centric" technologies, strategies, processes and mindsets to get their stakeholders inspired about their company, job, work and life. Moreover, they produce better performing people, teams and organizations. After all, don't you want to follow an energizing, transparent "social" leader who gets you motivated across all channels of communication (both the digital and the physical)? Sure you do. The good news is, the base qualities for good social leaders aren't uncommon? Frankly, they're pretty old-school; been required (or at least hoped for) leadership attributes for many decades. Indeed, they're not some new-fangled, pie-in-the-sky, born-on-the-web qualities that "older folks" can't get their heads around. Nope. Which is why everyone (especially those in leadership roles) can rally on being a social leader. If you think about it, all you really have to do is take your physical leadership capabilities, skills and actions (assuming you have some of those already) … and digitally sync them with today's social media/enterprise technologies. And do it now, if you're not already. Unless of course, you like to live with a bag over your head. Seriously: Start now. Get going. Do what you can. With what you have. Because you can't keep doing "business-as-usual" - or worse, wait it out, and hope it goes away (you've heard about the definition of insanity: doing the same thing over and over, and expecting different results). Heck, that's like waiting for Godot, and we all know what happened there.

The Co+Factor

will absolutely/positively generate a substantial

(quantitative and qualitative)

Return-On-Engagement.

And who doesn't like a good (and happy)

ROE?!

Who indeed?!

These pages left blank for
Notes, Ideas
&
Drawings
(Be Creative and Think Big!)

Mobile/Social Business & Systems of Engagement

(With special thanks to IBM® for their assistance.)

For the past decade, most technology innovation has centered on the consumer market; specifically – mobile devices, apps and social media. Today, hundreds of millions of consumers have integrated mobile/social apps and technologies into their daily lives. Shopping, playing, learning, communicating, and sharing experiences with family and friends – using a slew of mobile devices, apps and social/community platforms – are all a fun, easy and natural extension of our personal lives. For many, it's part of our DNA.

BUT THINK ABOUT PEOPLE'S WORK LIFE.

In the majority of organizations, employees continue to use the same (boring) infrastructure technology, that's been around for ages. For most, IT innovation (if there's even been innovation), has been centered on back-office strategies like SaaS, Managed Services and Cloud computing. And as far as end-users' goes, it's mostly been constrained to serving up the same old legacy enterprise software used on PCs, but now accessible (albeit not always functional) on mobile devices under the guise of BYOD. In other words, the IT most of us use at work, is outdated, not very enjoyable, and in big need of updating: both from a usability and productivity standpoint. Indeed, it's time to cross the divide between how we enjoy mobile and social technologies in our personal lives, with how we use mobile and social technologies to get work done. In time, enterprise "mobility" and "social" technologies will alter business as we know it.

The way, where and how we work, will change.

Soon … employees, customers, suppliers, partners and prospects … collaborating in cloud-based digital communities (social business) using high-speed mobile devices (enterprise mobility) … will reshape corporate environments. Eventually, every organization will need to embrace enterprise mobility and social business in order to communicate, collaborate and frankly, grow or survive.

THIS ISN'T FUTURISTIC; IT'S HAPPENING NOW.

The move to enterprise mobility and social business has begun. And according to experts, gross sales from products and services delivered through mobile/social will exceed $100B by 2020. In other words: big-time growth. Numbers aside – just imagine what corporate IT will look like in 2020, let alone 2025!? While it may not look like Star Trek, it won't look like it does today. There's no doubt that we're on the verge of a transformational (even revolutionary) enterprise computing era – where opportunity and challenge abound.

ENTERPRISE IN MOTION

Four powerful forces are converging. Social – unlocking new engines of innovation: your people, partners and customers. Mobile – knowing what value to put in people's hands. Cloud – the new way to drive growth, with less risk and investment. Analytics – the new way to turn all of the forces at work into competitive advantage. By 2020, because of the pervasive adoption of these technologies – new systems of people-centric engagement will be mainstream; and successful enterprises will be able to tap into shared insight, collective knowledge and expertise at the individual level to empower more meaningful engagement with both employees and customers

SYSTEMS OF ENGAGEMENT

There's an important transition taking place from inflexible, legacy IT "systems of record" – built around/for discrete pieces of information ("records") and geared towards transacting and passively providing information to a company's workers – to flexible, agile "systems of engagement", which are more decentralized, and leverage mobile/social technologies and platforms to encourage connectivity, collaboration and engagement inside and outside of the enterprise. When you compare systems of record

to systems of engagement, the differences and ramifications of those differences are significant. That said, the good news is, they should actually work together – even complement each other, as a matter of fact. And why do we need systems of engagement (to complement systems of record)? Because …

KNOWLEDGE IS BEING CREATED AND SHARED AT UNPRECEDENTED RATES

In just the last few years, Systems of Engagement has become a sweeping societal and economic phenomenon. People are now engaging, i.e. sharing original content, forming and joining virtual communities, organizing activities, tapping into the advice of others and sharing experiences – at scale and without boundaries. This collective knowledge is enabling people to rapidly learn, act with greater confidence and influence others in entirely new ways. In fact, digital engagement is now the #1 use of the internet, with 94% using it to learn, 78% to share knowledge and 49% to collaborate with experts

THE VIEWS AND ACTIVITIES OF PEOPLE ARE FAR MORE ACCESSIBLE

With the use of the mobile/social networking – the interactions among people, leaders and brands are now out in the open for everyone to see. This is creating a fundamentally new source of human data, enabling businesses to gain greater visibility into the sentiment, activities, performance and behaviors of large numbers of people. Importantly, the use of mobile/social has now evolved from a medium of personal interaction to an indispensable tool of business and commercial engagement. With 66% participating in professional communities, 81% engaging in brand conversations and 61% evaluating what others think and do, people are improving how they work and make decisions.

ORGANIZATIONS ARE FUNCTIONING WITH GREATER TRANSPARENCY

 With the open nature of today's business environment, where 70% of employees are engaged both internally and externally, organizations are working differently. In addition, with nearly everyone on the front lines building new relationships, the flow of information has become more difficult to contain. As their marketplaces and workplaces fuse together in entirely new ways, leaders are now prioritizing mutual trust, empowerment, responsiveness and authenticity as key attributes of a modern enterprise. In fact, 65% are now updating their organizational designs, policies, operating principles and business processes to best empower their people while protecting the enterprise.

THE NEW PRODUCTION LINE FOR THE KNOWLEDGE AGE

 Build distinctive expertise by enabling people to easily engage, learn, locate SMEs and access relevant information based on the collective knowledge of specialized communities.

Fuel client-centric innovation by crowdsourcing ideas, knowledge and resources from large-scale communities.

Improve productivity with collaborative models of communication and flattened organizational engagement.

Expand customer sales, loyalty and advocacy with exceptional digital experiences, providing access to expertise, the collective knowledge of your users and personalized value at every touch point.

THE NEW INTELLIGENCE FOR DRIVING BUSINESS OUTCOMES

 Apply a human face to workforce & marketplace data to better understand and proactively address behavioral, sentimental and performance-based trends.

Unlock stronger relationships by creating a more analytics-driven environment, personalized at every tough point, to optimize decision making, motivate action and empower people to act with greater confidence.

Optimize workforce talent by re-inventing how you recruit, motivate, improve and retain 'best fit' talent, using behavioral sciences, social analytics and comparative benchmarks – replacing guess-work with evidence-based decisions.

THE FUTURE OF HOW MODERN ENTERPRISES WORK

 Evolve your organizational design to embody a new style of leadership that facilitates a more collaborative, responsive, transparent and authentic way to work and engage with customers.

Create a culture of mutual trust that empowers people to engage and act, guided by social governance policies that employees understand, comply with and respect.

Socially enable your business processes with irresistible new capabilities that ease adoption and automate how your teams operate. Apply security and privacy controls built upon the flexibility of a mobile and cloud infrastructure.

EMPOWER PEOPLE

Activate Systems of Engagement for both customers and employees

Start with your workforce: Deploy an enterprise social platform across your workforce, integrating collaborative networking, knowledge management, social learning tools, expertise locators and workforce optimization applications. Integrate with the social web and your business processes.

Extend into the marketplace: Transform the customer experience across the spectrum of interaction. Use an integrated toolset that improves self-discovery, marketing effectiveness, online sales, service and loyalty programs. Underpin all interactions with social communities to energize advocacy networks and provide access to your expertise.

Adopt new crowdsourcing models: Deploy collaborative portals that manage crowdsourced methodologies and processes. Integrate these practices into your strategic planning processes, from product development, to marketing, to services and sales.

UNDERSTAND PEOPLE

Apply analytics to gain actionable insight from social data

Build a stronger workforce: Re-invent the discipline of human capital management by applying behavioral science across the talent lifecycle. Use evidence-based insights to attract, motivate and retain "best fit" talent, instilling a culture of self-awareness, self-improvement and stronger leadership.

Unlock actionable insights: Create new strategies to cultivate data-supported decision making, transform cultures and improve the effectiveness of how your workplace and marketplaces interact. Deploy data-driven methodologies, benchmarks and metrics, creating an action-oriented understanding of sentiment, behavior and performance.

Use data to engage with people as individuals, personalizing value at every touch point. Deploy new processes that help you better understand the unique characteristics, capabilities and preferences of your customers and employees, optimizing actions and loyalty.

TRUST PEOPLE

Pervasively harness a transparent and authentic way of working

Re-imagine your business design: Systematically evaluate how your organization works today and create a comprehensive yet evolutionary approach to implementing change. Design new leadership and operational policies with an eye on eased governance. Crowdsource employee input to best reflect your unique culture and way of working and to proactively educate and train your employees.

Enable your processes to be inherently social: Empower your people to easily evolve to a new way of working, by automating the adoption of social capabilities in the context of the business processes they already rely on to get work done. Deploy upon the flexibility of an open standards-based cloud and mobile infrastructure.

Protect the enterprise: Apply new security, privacy and compliance controls, enabling you to easily monitor, identify and preemptively address any regulatory issues, threats and/or inappropriate behavior that may occur.

PREPARING FOR THE FUTURE

 A challenge faced by virtually all enterprises in these turbulent times is how to build organizations that are more adaptive and agile, more creative and innovative, and more efficient and resilient. Increasingly, it is becoming clear that the traditional hierarchical enterprise, built on a structure of departments and a culture of compartmentalization, will give way to a socially synergistic enterprise built on continually evolving communities and a culture of sharing and innovation.

As such, we predict the path to becoming a Mobile/Social Business is inevitable. However, the differentiating factors – those which will separate the leaders from the masses – will stem from how effectively an organization embraces both a Mobile/Social culture as well as the technology to deepen customer relationships, drive operational efficiencies and optimize the workforce. And even the most successful organizations will encounter potholes along their paths. For example, in today's open world, disgruntled employees, partners and customers have a tremendous voice – something that must be considered as a business plots its Mobile/Social strategy. In addition, issues relating to protection of intellectual property in the socially networked world, as well as an enterprise's potential legal risks associated with social media, must be considered. Finally, HR policies likely need to evolve to take into account the massive increase in public information about employees, candidates and alumni. Despite the many issues to consider and the changes in organizational culture that must occur, enterprises can position themselves to enjoy deeper customer relationships, increased operational efficiency and an optimized workforce. Organizations that leverage a Mobile/Social culture and technology framework (not to mention The Co+Factor) have the potential to transform themselves and take leadership roles in their markets and industries.